York Between the Wars

Captured on film by
Donald Gaddes Sheldon
(1893 - 1952)
with introduction and captions by
Michael Pocock

Highgate Publications (Beverley) Limited, 1993

British Library Cataloguing in Publication Data available

Copyright © 1993 The Sheldon Collection of Photographs

Highgate Publications (Beverley) Ltd., 24 Wylies Road, Beverley, HU17 7AP
Telephone (0482) 866826

Printed by
Colourspec, Unit 7, Tokenspire Park, Hull Road, Woodmansey, Beverley, HU17 0TB
Telephone (0482) 864264

ISBN 0 948929 69 3

Introduction

'York is not conscious of its beauty like so many ancient towns: it is too old and too wise and too proud to trick itself out for the admiration of tourists. That is one of the many reasons why I love it and its little country-town streets.'

H.V. Morton, writing in 1926, gives the true feel of the York of these pictures. It was a country town and cathedral city, existing only for its citizens, for the folk from the surrounding villages who came to buy and sell and for the clergy of the Minster.

Its way of life was reflected in the numerous, high-class shops — Grisedale's, Leak and Thorpe's, Rowntree's, and W.P. Brown's for clothing and draperies — Border's, Thompson's, Barton's, Scott's and Wright's for foodstuffs of the top quality. My parents lived in Acomb from 1912 to 1917, when it was a country village. Returning to York for a visit during a holiday to Scarborough in 1930, my mother was shocked to see the refined atmosphere of Coney Street challenged by the arrival of Woolworth's — 'Nothing over sixpence in the stores,' as it brashly proclaimed in gold letters on a red background. In the Coney Street of 1993 Woolworth's is positively 'established', nor can you buy anything in it for 2½p.

Students of social history and people of my age who can remember, think of the inter-war years in terms of the slump (not tactfully passed off as a 'recession'), of the means test, the dole queues and the marches. Those who were there at the time tell me that there was nothing like that in York. The railways, the chocolate firms, and other local employers of labour were not affected by the depression, or not to any great extent, and unemployment was not a problem, though, of course, the railwaymen would be involved in the General Strike of 1926. On the other hand, young workers of today would regard the deprived life-style of their working class grandparents as intolerable.

Yet the young people of the time, having only their own world as a measure, certainly had a good time in it. For entertainment there was the Theatre Royal, the Empire, where Gracie Fields performed on occasion, and at least seven cinemas. (This was the number when I was stationed at Strensall in '42.) There were Balls at the Assembly Rooms and less formal dances at the De Grey Rooms and on the upper floor of what is now Fairfax House. In the summer there were excursions to the coast by 'chara' or train. Those returning from Scarborough by the latter who had omitted to buy tickets left the train unofficially when it slowed down on the home stretch in the Bootham area.

For moving around York there had been a tram service from 1878, first horse-drawn — then, from 1906, electric. The service extended from Dringhouses to Fulford and Clifton. Hardy, and car-less inhabitants of Tadcaster and the neighbouring villages cycled to the Cross Keys, left their bikes there until their return, and boarded the tram. In 1935 buses replaced trams as a result of a contract between York Corporation and the

West Yorks Road Car Company. Those who remember the period believe that both the buses and the trams before them gave a more frequent and reliable service than is operated today.

A feature of York since Roman times has been its garrison, and a social event of the twenties and thirties was Military Sunday, traditionally in May. On this day all the regiments stationed in York marched with their bands from their particular barracks to the Minster, watched by crowds from every vantage point. At that time the liberal establishment had not yet hi-jacked the C.of E. and it was not politically correct to regard the service of God and the King as mutually incompatible.

Several photographs in this book show policemen directing hardly life-threatening traffic or keeping order at a gala by sitting, unarmed and unprotected, on a horse and chatting to the passers-by. This reflects the peaceful nature of the times and the absence of any crime wave. True, the 'Bobby' at Dringhouses was said to push inconvenient drunks over the 'frontier' at the Chase to be dealt with by his opposite number in the York Force. True, one party of carol singers was in receipt of a bucket of cold water from a well-wisher, but generally things were pretty calm. However, we should not fall for the 'Golden Age' myth. The fights in Micklegate, the banning of known trouble-makers from a range of York pubs and the arrests for drug offences show that York in 1993 is a more violent place than York in 1933 but certainly less violent than in the 1850's when George Hudson's strong-armed men furthered his political career with chicory knives. It is not a case of things going from bad to worse but moving in a circle.

The main contrast between the York of the photographs and the York of today can be illustrated by an old lady's memory of August Bank Holidays. In our time the shop-keepers regard the festival as one of the busiest and most prosperous of their year. In the twenties the city centre was empty because all the York folk were enjoying themselves elsewhere and none of the outsiders were coming to enjoy themselves in York.

That which is within the lifetime, and even the adult lifetime, of living men can become history if the earlier society is recognisably different from that of today. This happens if changes are rapid or profound. It happened after the First War through changes in what men believed and how they thought. The Somme was the watershed. It has happened, to a lesser extent, after the Second War, not through psychological changes but changes in technology leading to a different kind of life at a material level. We can see this if we look at these pictures and think of 'now'.

Michael Pocock
September 1993.

Shopping in Stonegate

Stonegate has been described as one of the prettiest luxury shopping streets in the world. Shoppers, however, can no longer drive along the street, pedestrianised in 1971, as shown in this photograph.

Can we afford it?

Window shopping in Stonegate, October 1922.

Room to move in pre-tourist York

Visitors today would hardly recognize the quiet empty street as the modern bustling Stonegate.

'Summer Suns are glowing'

The deep shadow of the street contrasts with the bright sun shining on the pale stone of the Minster. Parking obviously no problem!

'Like us they lived'

York is a paradise for antique and curio collectors. This couple have discovered an Aladdin's Cave in Ousegate — with prices far cheaper than today's.

'Twelve o'clock and all's well' — we hope!

A peaceful night in Micklegate.

'So she said to me...'

John William Collier was a butcher at 8 Shambles throughout the twenties and thirties.

Where do we go from here?

Spectators always gather to watch men at work but hats and caps are no longer the norm.

'Willing people — those willing to work and those willing to let them'

Road repairs in a side street off Bootham. Children were sometimes sent to inhale the tar fumes to cure 'chestiness'.

September Afternoon

Bootham 'crowded with traffic' — by the standard of the time.

'O Worship The Lord in the beauty of holiness' — York Minster: west front

In 627 Paulinus, a missionary from Rome, converted Edwin, King of Northumbria, and built a wooden church where the Minster now stands. It is likely that he chose the site deliberately, that of the old headquarters of the legion, to associate the new religion with the prestige that the Roman Empire still enjoyed, even among the barbarians. There were several later churches in wood or stone, and the last Saxon one was accidentally burnt down in the fighting between the Normans and Saxons in 1069. Thomas of Bayeux, the newly appointed Norman Archbishop, built a Norman-style building, the remains of which can be seen in the undercroft. The Minster as we see it today was built between 1227 and 1472. We can marvel at the skill of the stone masons, the carpenters and the glaziers, but should also spare a thought for the labourers and the hours of back-breaking toil with rafts and rope and oxen to get the stone from Jackdaw Crag in Tadcaster to the pinnacles at the top of the towers. Where an ancient church or cathedral is called a minster the reason is that it was not only used as a place of worship but as a centre for scholars studying the Scriptures and the early writings of the Church. York was such a centre and famous among scholars throughout Europe.

Sermon in Stones — York Minster: the south-west Bell Tower

Early medieval bells were cast on the spot. A window in the Minster was donated by a York bell founder and commemorates the life of St. William. The great clock bell, known as Great Peter of York, was cast in London and was the largest in the country until Big Ben was installed at Westminster.

Roofs of old York

Donald Sheldon, the photographer, had an eye for the unusual and here he was attracted by the contrast between the vertical lines of the Minster and the complex diagonal pattern of the roofs. Note the evidence of coal fires and the absence of television aerials.

Mists of Autumn

Here Donald Sheldon, was obviously intrigued by the contrast between the sharp foreground and the mist-shrouded Minster.

Hold on tight!

Choirboys on the central tower of the Minster. Caps were worn at all times!

On top of the Minster

Compare the formal dress of these visitors on the roof of the Minster with the informality of today's track-suits and trainers.

The Ouse, the Humber, the North Sea...and beyond — the port of York

From the disintegration of the Roman road system to the coming of the railways after 1830 heavy goods were moved by water. Thus a river was a source of wealth to a town. The Angles, the Vikings and the men of the Middle Ages had wharfs and warehouses along the Ouse, and the Corporation received a good income from tolls on shipping. Sea-going ships sailed from York until the later years of the 18th century, while today barge traffic flourishes, including the delivery of newsprint for the *Yorkshire Evening Press*.

The day's work

Scene on the wharf side near Ouse Bridge.

Hard work on a cold day

Rescuing an ice-bound boat from the River Ouse.

Manpower — young people boating on the Ouse

Kenneth Grahame, through Ratty, declared that, 'There is nothing, absolutely nothing, to compare with messing about in boats.' Given the river, York in the twenties and thirties attracted the amateur oarsman, and still does.

'The Boyhood of Raleigh' updated

A boat-load of boys on the Ouse opposite the Guildhall.

'Hope springs eternal...'

Fishing on the Ouse. Trilbies, ties and school caps even for fishing!

An English Summer — a pleasure boat on the Ouse

The boat is probably taking trippers for a view of the Archbishop's Palace at Bishopthorpe. Originally the Archbishops lived in a palace in the Minster park but moved out to get away from the smoke, smell and general unpleasantness of a crowded medieval city. The arches of the original palace can be seen in the Minster ground and have been incorporated in a memorial to the 14th Army.

My Kingdom for a Boat!

The Ouse in flood — still a regular hazard. There was bad flooding in York in three consecutive years in the thirties. *The Yorkshire Gazette* described that on 4 January 1930 as 'the worst for 40 years', and there was more serious flooding on 11 September 1931 and 27 May 1932.

Food and Water

Donald Sheldon had a talent for capturing on film the fleeting moment. This apparently simple 'shot' is, in fact, a sophisticated composition with the lamp standard cleverly used in the foreground.

'The grist of the slow-ground ages' — the Guildhall from Lendal Bridge

Ancient cities acquired the right to self-government through charters granted by kings. York had a mayor by the name of Nigel in the reign of Stephen and, as it is unlikely that a charter would be issued in the midst of civil war and baronial anarchy, it is probable that York's original charter was granted in the reign of Henry I (1100-1135). The original Council Chamber was on Ouse Bridge. The present Guildhall was built between 1446 and 1461. It was badly damaged by enemy action in the last war and has been restored.

Gilding the Lily — repairing Skeldergate Bridge

From the days of Eboracum, York, one city on two sides of a river, needed a bridge to be viable. The Roman bridge was in the vicinity of the Guildhall. From the coming of the Angles to Tudor times the bridge was a wooden one, on the site of the present Ouse Bridge. This wooden bridge was rebuilt in stone when the original structure was carried away in a storm in the winter of 1564-5. The stone bridge was widened and the gradient reduced early in the 19th century. To meet greater industrial activity arising out of the development of the railways Lendal Bridge was opened in 1863. The imitation turret, now a shop and cafe, was the original toll bar. Tolls were abolished in 1894. The top six inches of the iron parapet had to be added to meet safety regulations when the height of the roadway was raised to take a tram-track. Skeldergate Bridge was opened in 1881.

Scene of Peace, Memories of Battle

Bootham Bar survived its threatened demolition in 1832 when the barbican was pulled down. Horse-drawn transport is still seen in the centre of York, but now carrying tourists, not goods.

Midnight
— Midwinter

A view through Bootham Bar showing the lower end of the raised portcullis. Another subtle composition of contrasting lines and curves, with the arch acting as a frame and interest found even in the tyre tracks on the snow.

Winter Scene — Bootham Bar

In the bustling modern City of York it would be almost impossible to capture this tranquil scene. Notice how snow sharpens and highlights the stones on the bar, the plants and the railings.

Walking through history — Fishergate Bar

The original Fishergate Bar was blocked up as a result of damage during a riot in the reign of Henry VII (1485-1509). The gate was re-opened in 1836 for the convenience of those using the cattle market.

One more springtime — Micklegate Bar in April

A peaceful place in the years between the Wars but one that had seen more than its fair share of violence. It was here that the heads of criminals executed for high treason were once displayed.

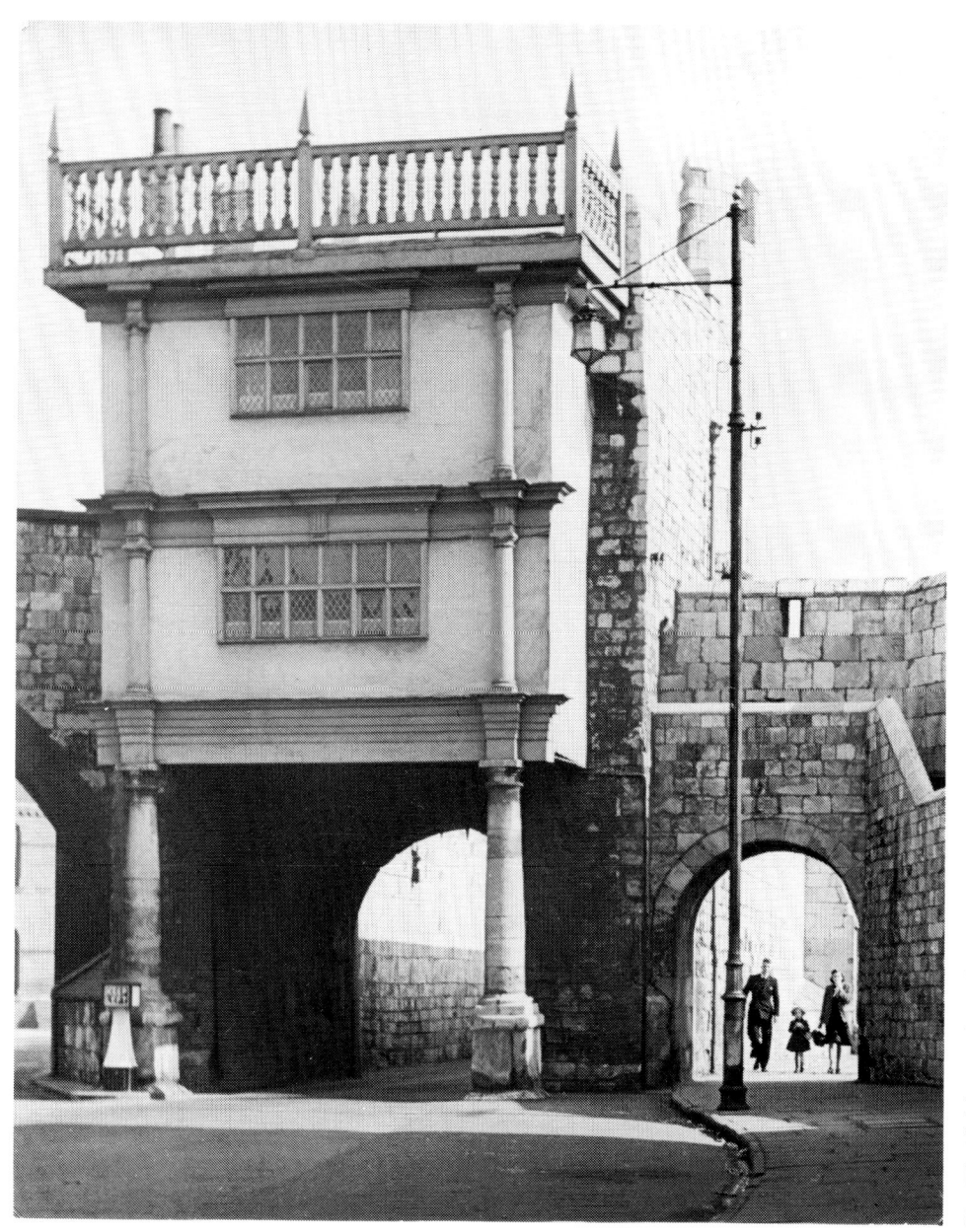

'Des. Res.'— Walmgate Bar

The house was built on to Walmgate Bar between 1584 and 1586. John Brown, artist and historian of York, was born in this house in 1793. Originally all Bars had barbicans — the bit built out at the front — but only that of Walmgate Bar survives.

Through here for Scarborough and the beach

Monk Bar had had its portcullis dropped in 1914, the first time in 300 years. In the 1920's excavations started in the area. Notice the newspaper seller on the left standing on the road — a great contrast with modern York.

Behind the scenes — the winding gear for the portcullis in Monk Bar

The portcullis of an ancient gateway or castle was let down at night or when an attack was expected. The one in Bootham is a replica but that in Monk Bar is the original. It was last used when it was lowered during the Coronation celebrations in 1953 but the experiment is not likely to be repeated. Lowering it was alright but getting it up again was a different matter!

Britain's Heritage in Stone — the white wall of old York, near Monk Bar

The York walls from Baile Hill to the Ouse and on the other side of the river to the Foss at Layerthorpe Bridge were built in the first half of the 13th century. From the Red Tower to the Foss at Fishergate Tower the walls date from a century later. In this area the ground was marshy and full of clay pits so that siege engines could not be used in an attack. Therefore the walls did not need to be as high as on the Bootham side. The gap between Layerthorpe Bridge and the Red Tower was filled by a lake — the King's Fish Pool — made by damming the Foss.

York's Defences — Fishergate Postern

'No mean city' — York from the City walls

Inter-war elegance with near-empty streets, horse-drawn transport, and iron railings round well-trimmed lawns.

1259 and still standing - Clifford's Tower

William the Conqueror built two castles to hold down York. The one on the site of Clifford's Tower was so badly damaged in the anti-Jewish riot of 1190 as to be untenable. The present tower was therefore built between 1245 and 1259. The Cliffords were an old Yorkshire family but their connection with the Tower is unknown. The name, Clifford's Tower, was not used until the 16th century.

Heartbreak House — verse to be seen on the wall of the Debtors' Prison

> This Prison is a House of Care
> A Grave For Man Alive
> A Touch Stone To Try A Friend
> No Place For Man To Thrive

Until well into the 19th century debt was regarded as a crime to be punished by imprisonment until the debt was paid. Since the prisoner had little chance of raising the money he was in a worse case than the robber or other convict with a limited sentence.

The Toll of Centuries — the doorway of St. William's College before restoration

St. William's College was built by Archbishop Neville in the later 15th century as a house for chantry priests. These were employed to say masses for the soul of the founder of the chantry who had left money for this purpose. In Neville's opinion these priests were under-employed and badly behaved and needed to be re-housed under stricter discipline where he could keep an eye on them. He therefore built the College. It was called after St. William, a former Archbishop of York. When he was entering the city to be enthroned, Ouse Bridge collapsed under the weight of the spectators who were sitting on it, and the fact that no one was drowned was taken to be a miracle, supporting the canonisation of William by the Pope. Having a Saint buried there increased the number of pilgrims to the Minster, which was probably why the Dean and Chapter recommended William to the Pope in the first place.

Tycoons of the Middle Ages — the undercroft of the Merchant Adventurers' Hall

Traders right up to the 18th century formed companies to strengthen their hands in getting good terms from their own kings and from foreign rulers and for protection against pirates and bandits. Medieval guilds also combined the functions of insurance companies, dining clubs, religious congregations, maintaining trading standards and undertaking charitable work for members.

York Water Tower

With the portcullis down and the walls manned, York could still be attacked by boat from the river, either up or down stream. To meet this threat towers were built where the walls came down to the river by the present Lendal Bridge and in the vicinity of Skeldergate Bridge. In each tower there was a windlass, and, fastened to it, a chain which lay along the bed of the river. At night, or in times of danger, the 'chain men' in each tower wound up the chains until they stretched taut from bank to bank, barring the way to hostile craft.

Ring out the old

Is this Holy Trinity Church, King's Court, demolished in 1937? As public worship declined in this century ancient York churches could no longer be supported by congregations, and many, as shown above, were demolished. This has now been halted in the interests of conservation of ancient and beautiful buildings, and redundant churches are maintained and used for social purposes *e.g.* leisure centres for old people.

'Mak all t' railways come to York': reputedly said by George Hudson — York Station

On 3 December 1833 George Hudson, a York draper of country stock, addressed a group of businessmen on the subject of a railway from York. The railway, running to Selby and connected with other early lines by Leeds, was opened on 29 May 1839. From that date York was a railway town in its own right and a key point in the railway system of Britain.

'This way, please' — Point Duty

Donald Sheldon was attracted by the photographic potential of these York street scenes, but today much of the interest lies in the contrast they show with modern traffic conditions.

The Roaring (?) Twenties — traffic control in 1928

Order was maintained in York, as in other ancient cities, by the Watch, consisting of old retired soldiers, notorious for their inefficiency. In 1829 Sir Robert Peel introduced modern policing in central London. This idea reached York in 1836. A London adviser recommended a force of three sergeants and 20 constables. York Corporation, with an eye to costs, settled for one sergeant and 12 constables as 'sufficient for so moral and religious a city as York'.

Old Wood, Ancient Stone and New Metal — a car entering the old gateway opposite All Saints, Pavement

A car entering the old gateway opposite All Saints, Pavement. Who was the owner of KH 7672? The windscreen was wound open to aid ventilation on hot days.

The Heart of York — view of the Minster

Another subtle study combining natural features, buildings, a vehicle and people: the inanimate and animate elements which create the atmosphere of a cathedral city such as York.

Weighing-up the odds — Knavesmire Gala Races

The vale of York breeds good horses, and since Tudor times men have raced them. From 1530 there was an annual race through the Forest of Galtres, the winner getting a golden bell, which he kept for a year, and a sum of money which did not last as long. In August 1714 the King's Cup was run for the first time. In 1731 the race course was moved to the Knavesmire and in 1754 the grandstand was built.

No bets on this horse

York people have always loved horses — on and off the course. The Knavesmire has also been the venue for many social events. On 3 September 1938, for example, there was a theatrical fête.

'Reach for the sky' — hot air balloon at York Gala

After 1939 balloons had a rather different significance.

Dedication — artist at work

Note the spats. York is still a magnet to artists — and even more to photographers.

Amateurs and Professionals — Russian guns captured in the Crimean War, displayed in St. George's Field

Did the soldiers — and the boys — see real action in the war that brought the thirties to a violent end?

54

R.I.P. - Cholera Burial Ground

The Cholera epidemic took place in 1832 and the victims were buried in a plot near the station both because it was suspected that the graves might be a source of infection and because of the overcrowded condition of the traditional churchyards within the City walls. A beginning was made on a modern system of brick sewers and in 1836 a City cemetery run by a private company was opened in Fulford.

'I am the Resurrection and the Life' — York Minster from the Cholera Burial Ground